PENGUIN BOOKS

Poor

Advance Praise

'Caleb Femi is a gift to us all from the storytelling gods. He is a poet of truth and rage, heartbreak and joy. But above all, this is love poetry. Love of community, language, music and form. This book flows from the fabric of boyhood to the politics and architecture of agony, from the material to the spiritual, always moving, always real. *Poor* is the heartbeat of a living city which truly knows itself. Caleb is a mighty and positive force in UK culture and this is a vital book' Max Porter, author of *Grief is the Thing with Feathers* and *Lanny*

'In this fabulous debut, concrete becomes a paradox of toughness and vulnerability, confinement and shelter . . . Caleb Femi's riveting photographs and compassionate yet hard-hitting lines map North Peckham's black boys and blocks . . . His depictions of young black men possess a brother's empathy . . . It's simply stunning. Every image is a revelation' Terrance Hayes, author of *American Sonnets for My Past and Future Assassin*

'Mesmerizing and transporting. I've never read a collection like this . . . I literally had to shake off the experience once I was finished. [This] incredible collection . . . gives voice to a London many would prefer to ignore . . . I don't think it possible for anyone to come away from this book without having developed new levels of empathy and compassion' Derek Owusu, author of *That Reminds Me*

'Impressive . . . These lyrical lamentations and praise poems seek to illuminate the reality for the mandem in the endz. Femi's rhapsodic, elegiac verses magnify the connections between the architectural design of inner-city tower blocks and the behaviour of their inhabitants . . . At the heart of the collection is the poet's deconstruction of language, fusing biblical cadence with a contemporary street vernacular. There is something reminiscent of

William Blake's visionary poetic in Femi's commitment to a realistic worship for places like Aylesbury Estate and North Peckham, as well as their communities . . . [recalls] Gwendolyn Brooks's and Nate Marshall's odes to Chicago . . . [*Poor* is] in conversation with Roger Robinson's and Jay Bernard's poems of witness and poetic gospel, which . . . create myths, legends, and folklore that render black bodies as holy' Malika Booker, author of *Pepper Seed*

'Caleb Femi's *Poor* bristles with the exhilarations and violences of boyhood and adolescence. In its interplay of image and text, of photographic image and poetic image, the book asks us to consider what is seen and unseen, spoken of and concealed; what is, in one of many numinous phrases, "proof of light". More than this, these are poems of witness, both noun and verb: poems of the self and what the self can bear' Stephen Sexton, author of *If All the World and Love Were Young*

'Giving a mythic resonance to communal life, the poems in Caleb Femi's *Poor* are vital, confronting and electric. Political, spiritual, formally inventive and energized by a music of protest and grief, this is a rare and anthemic debut' Seán Hewitt, author of *Tongues of Fire*

'I am reading a powerful book of poetry by a young man, Caleb Femi. Oh my God, he has a book called *Poor* and he's just stirring me. Destroying me. I look up to him as a poet' Michaela Coel, creator and writer of *I May Destroy You*

ABOUT THE AUTHOR

Raised on the North Peckham estate in South London, Caleb Femi is a poet and director who uses film, photography and music to explore the boundaries of poetry on the page, in performance and in digital media. He has written and directed short films for the BBC and Channel 4, and poems for Tate Modern, the Royal Society for Literature, St Paul's Cathedral, the BBC, the *Guardian* and more. He has been featured in the Dazed 100 list of the next generation shaping youth culture. From 2016 to 2018, he served as the Young People's Laureate for London. This is his first collection.

CALEB FEMI

Poor

PENGUIN BOOKS

PENGUIN BOOKS

UK | USA | Canada | Ireland | Australia
India | New Zealand | South Africa

Penguin Books part of the Penguin Random House group of companies
whose addresses can be found at global.penguinrandomhouse.com

First published 2020

001

Copyright © Caleb Femi, 2020

Set in 10/13.75 pt Warnock Pro
by Integra Software Services Pvt. Ltd, Pondicherry
Printed in Italy by Printer Trento S.r.l.

A CIP catalogue record for this book is available from the British Library

ISBN: 978–0–141–99215–0

www.greenpenguin.co.uk

My people humble people who expect / Nothing
                                          – T. S. Eliot

As a consequence of which, they must
find money by these means

                                          – Darcus Howe

If I die now, my mum got bumped by the juju man
                                          – J Hus

CONTENTS

I

Barter

Give me your face
& I'll give you mine
Give me your benefit of the doubt
& I'll give you my doubt of innocence
Give me your milk
& I'll give you my sand
Give me your neat nails
& I'll give you my exoskeleton

I think I know where to find
my mother's mother's kin
scattered like dust mite in the wind
If I gather them all   will you take them
& give me your pristine family tree
The steely chic of my block
is nice this time of year   you are
welcome to stay there if
I can stay in your home
I mean your small
holiday home in Costa Blanca

Once I pulled my tonsil out of my mouth
with my thumb and index finger
I was reaching for my voice box
I rarely use it to its full potential
I would say   its condition
is nearly brand new   take it
for when you need to rap hiphop songs

I am a superhero with the power of invisibility
problem is I haven't quite got the handle of it yet

at the worst times   I become invisible
at the worst times   I become visible

I loved a girl so much it eroded my skin
I loved her until she swelled to her brink
I loved her so much that one night during sex
I cried & my tears nearly filled up to the ceiling
& she   not being able to swim   drowned

Honeytrap & Likkle Bwoi

What-what do you know about mercy?
The likkle bwoi from the endz know it be
the last thing you plead when the dust settles.
What do you know about this story – the full of it?
When the single cloud was moving at the pace of wisdom
they called Tasha 'set-up chick', but the truth
was that the likkle bwoi was an arrogant fool.
We would need a new set of images to map
what happened – off endz, caught slipping, six opps –
but first, tell me what you know
about Reebok classics, Dipset, sovereign rings,
aquamasters, flexing? This has nothing to do with nostalgia
but to access the story you must take yourself back
to the last time you heard a scream that didn't signal rain,
out the belly of the likkle bwoi, blue with running,
with shiny rubber limbs, playing likkle bwoi games.
The hands of his laughing scream feeling the walls
the way bats converse with the dark world.
You know dem way there?
When the afternoon carried one atomic intent,
horny likkle bwoi playing horny likkle games,
baking in laughter like he be the first to be horny in history,
forgetting how he came to be born (you know dem way there?),
dashing round the estate trying not to get seen
by dem eyes that love to snitch. Anyway, the story
started with a text: *Tasha's your cuz?*
she's peng / gimme her number?
And maybe Tasha *was* peng
or maybe her skin was just light like she was plated in gold.

Likkle bwoi trying to get up in her panties
ain't got a clue what to do if he got up in dem panties
— you know dem way there?

A Designer Talks of a Home /
A Resident Talks of Home (I)

00:00:00   we spend 87 percent of our lives inside buildings

00:00:34   *I was conceived within these walls in '87*

00:01:09   how they are designed really affects how we feel

00:07:53   *the wallpaper was here before me, I don't claim it*

00:01:43   how we behave

00:08:13   *Mum says this is a good home. When I was little I used
           to peel the yellow from the wallpaper*

00:01:56   design is not just a visual thing; it's a thought process

00:12:12   *once I swallowed an apple pip & a guy from the 12th
           floor told me*

00:02:20   it's a skill . . .

00:14:02   *an apple tree will grow out from my belly*

00:02:39   design is a tool to enhance our humanity. . . a frame
           for life

00:15:45   *don't that mean I will be the first treeboy on the estate?*

00:02:50   putting the human experience at the beginning of
           the process

00:17:39   *the guy said trees live as long as boys do here that's*
                  why we have concrete

00:03:32   tactile memory

00:18:01   *at the back of our block there is a wall full of RIPs . . .*
                  a thousand unlived lives of boys & trees

00:03:46   empathy is the cornerstone of design

00:18:50   *y'know the architect that designed this estate killed*
                  himself

00:03:53   it's all about showmanship and theatricality

00:19:20   *Mum reckons that's why they covered the rot with*
                  cladding

00:04:01   it's about how things feel & smell as much as how
                  they look

00:20:15   *'cause concrete smells like a siege . . . when it rains*
                  I like to

00:04:23   imbue people with a sense of wellbeing,
                  empowerment, gentle joyfulness

00:21:09   *pretend I live*

00:04:56   translate the future life of a building into design
                  language

00:22:23   *on the 19th floor you can see everything but the future*

00:05:03   those great long corridors reduced people

00:23:59   *we see the same view even when we're not looking,*
             we're usually not looking

00:05:25   to see that a building could have such an impact
             on the way people felt, on the way they interacted

00:25:48   *at the scene we know who did it . . . keep our*
             mouths shut when boydem come with their

00:09:13   it's about interrogation and empathy

00:26:03   *[laughter]*

00:09:58   materials are the things that tell the truth

00:27:29   *if these walls could talk our ears would bleed.*

00:10:17   humans are naturally drawn to the material

00:28:32   *is fire a material?*

00:13:03   we discover the world through our senses

00:29:10   *some animals only map the world through one*
             sense . . . & so can survive smoke

00:13:54   our materials speak to us

00:30:02   *concrete makes me feel safe . . . when I leave my*
             block I don't feel safe

Put Them in the Room of Spirit
& Slow Time

Boys who know roadside sun
      & know where to find fruiting lamp posts.

Boys who were raised on the empty shell of a fridge
      who sit with rocks in their stomachs and laugh.

Boys who feel like Halloween costumes,
      who wear winter coats in summer heat.

Boys who do road, actually *do* road
      – ten toes on an opp block road.

Boys who don't go to the corner shop on their ones
      because of *boydem* or boys like them.

Boys who felt grief and its economies of scale
      in the budget of burial.

Boys who look to polar bears for lessons
      on how to grow white fur on black skin.

Boys who always swear they're five minutes away,
      who know that time is a promise of smoke.

Boys who know that a wheel-up bar in a Grime rave
      is a loop of better days to come.

Boys whose names sound like the rip of duct tape
      or the boom of a twelfth bell.

Boys who sleep in cupboards
     & in back seats of burning cars.

Boys who can't explain why they flinch
     at the knock of a door.

Boys who live by the code
     & stay sealed up with wax.

Boys who stopped waiting for a spirit in a holy place
     & stopped breaking for morning.

Boys in search of a hyperbolic time chamber
     where their clutch of years pours slow.

Chirpse

All the girls we know
call us trouble, but the
good kind call us annoying
but really mean: *rosé*
which really means: *kiss me
entirely*. This pretty picture I paint
is not the whole truth:
in the streets where we hold
like heavy water, cutting
the stone of pavement,
we call the girls we know
as if we never knew them,

as if we were reading a diagram
out loud:

         – *Bi*g *batty*
         – *Braids*
         – *Bress*   – *Ting*
         – *Yat*

– *Flesh*. In response
they don't call us anything.
They know we will see them
later on, the *big batty, braids,
bress,* in our mothers
who bring home our favourite cereal
as they always have.

Because Of The Times

*North Peckham estate is the best documented and the most notorious
. . . 65 multi-storey blocks all on a 40-acre site, comprising 1444 homes.
This was linked to a wide pedestrian deck . . . forming a network of ways
containing housing, shops and other facilities . . . Residents . . . could 'walk
freely along this two and a half miles of deck away from the . . . traffic.'*

   – Municipal Dreams in Housing, London

Brown and gold and stretched like the slurring
of a toothless drunk. Sweet-neighbour talk
coined it a mega-estate. Your flat was in the north:
one bedroom and seven bodies making do.
You told yourself it was a small alcove
set beyond the reach of the clock's hands.

On Mondays the detergent they used to clean
the stairs smelled of bubblegum; so you would
walk through the corridors that connected
one block to another block, one joy
to another joy: a system of nerves,
a casing of sand, and endless windows.

Is this what the architect had in mind?
A paradise of affordable bricks, tucked under
a blanket, shielded from the world –
all that hopeful good on powder-blue paper,
measured lines defining angles
of respite for the poor. What foresight he had

to put shops and launderettes on the estate
so mothers could send their children on errands
knowing that even if they walked a mile

their fawny ankles wouldn't ever set foot
on open ground, to be lost to the city's
clutches, or feel the affliction of rain.

How quickly rain dried, how loudly bricks
hummed again as you went back to your life,
your tinkering, your blooming, making-do.
Nothing the estate raised was a monster, yet
the devil found good ground to plough his seeds.
GABOS – the widening gyre. Residents on the brink:

washed, wrung, walking shrines asking questions
to which the architect maintained that their design
was a good solution because of the times.
It is true on paper there were no designs for a tomb
yet the East wing stairs were where Damilola was found:
blue dawn, blue body, blue lights, blue tapes.

Thirteen

You will be four minutes from home
when you are cornered by an officer
who will tell you of a robbery, forty
minutes ago in the area. *You fit
the description of a man?* – You'll laugh.
Thirteen, you'll tell him: you're thirteen.

You'll be patted on the shoulder, then, by another fed
whose face takes you back to Gloucester Primary School,
a Wednesday assembly about *being little stars.*
This same officer had an horizon in the east
of his smile when he told your class that
you were all *supernovas,*
the biggest and brightest stars.

You will show the warmth of your teeth
praying he remembers the heat of your supernova;
he will see you powerless – plump.
You will watch the two men cast lots for your organs.

Don't you remember me? you will ask.
You gave a talk at my primary school.
While fear condenses on your lips,
you will remember that Wednesday, after the assembly,
your teacher speaking more about supernovas:
how they are, in fact, dying stars
on the verge of becoming black holes.

II

Concrete (I)

I have nothing to offer you
but my only pair of Air Max 90s.
In principle, they are my autopsy laid out
in rubber and threading. Take with them
God's speed through the valley of days
low yielding in laughs when the grey of
the concrete is louder than your outfit.
I know it can only do so much to cloak you
from *boydem* so keep this in mind:

You don't have to run faster than the police –
you just have to run faster than the slowest person.

Slip the slope of your ankle into the canvas:
may it lift you up seven feet tall so that
they know a lighthouse is on the endz;
and when you walk, walk proud,
for you walk in what I might have been.

Collective Noun: A Play by an Onlooker

After Suzan-Lori Parks

Characters: SHOP CCTV CAM 1 (sees blind spots)
& SHOP CCTV CAM 2 (sees open spots).

Setting: a corner shop in Dalston; both cameras positioned at opposite ends.

A boy is chased into the corner shop by Policemen & is tackled on the side aisle. Two officers are on top of the boy when:

SHOP CCTV CAM 1: Lemme ask ya su'thin.
SHOP CCTV CAM 2: Go on ask me su'thin.
SHOP CCTV CAM 1: If a group of Pandas is called an embarrassment.
SHOP CCTV CAM 2: Yah.
SHOP CCTV CAM 1: Wha duya call a group of pigs chokin' a boy on the floor?
SHOP CCTV CAM 2: 'pends on the boy.
SHOP CCTV CAM 1: 'pends on the pigs.
SHOP CCTV CAM 2: His body.
SHOP CCTV CAM 1: The weight?
SHOP CCTV CAM 2: Yah, the weight of his colour.

SHOP CCTV CAM 1:
SHOP CCTV CAM 2:

Curtain.

Coping

Dark skin boys scare everything in the dark
though really
we're just trying to scare away the dark.

Round here this is how we greet each other:
What's good, my g?
as if to say, *Are you safe, my g?*

Isn't this how you would call out to your friends
if you too were in a dark place,
standing on a ledge?

Shoutout to us boys who play out here.
God knows how we do it.
Maybe God doesn't know –

maybe an estate, tall as it is,
is the half-buried femur of a dead god,
and the blue light of dawn

– his son in mourning –
looks on the things we do
when there is one less boy among us.

How we pour the holy spirit out of the bottle
onto the concrete where his ashes lie,
stir it into a clay, mould it into a new body

and like a kite in fading wind
watch his soul sink back to good earth,
settle into his body like he never left.

Isn't this what you would do for your friends
if you too were in a dark place,
standing on the edge?

Things I Have Stolen

From the highest shelf
my tiptoes could reach me
I stole a Mars bar & Haribo sweets.
It wasn't a big deal: Mum said
their prices were a robbery anyway.

Later years, Marusha stole my heart,
jerked it out through the ribcage.
In desperation I stole another,
then another. Then a few more:
Fatima, Rihanna, Andrea.
Better to have and not need, I thought,
than need and not have.

Aylesbury estate, I saw Kevin steal Frank's
white Air Force Ones. Do you know how long
it takes a fourteen-year-old yout to save
enough Ps to buy those trainers?
Kevin stole Frank's soul, plucked it
like fruit in a swaying tree.

And I thought, what a game changer:
if Kevin can steal a soul, what else can be stolen?
So I stole the flavour from water
and I stole the solar eclipse.

Then I stole my torn name from the mouth
of the policeman who stops
and searches me
every week. Stole hunger pangs
from underneath our bed, at night.

Six years went by. At Kevin's funeral
I reached into the air
and stole the family's grief.

A Slow History of a Quick Death

I swallow an apple whole at the till of a newsagent
before *Bossman* has the chance to call me a thief.

He reaches down my throat for his silver, pulls out
a muleta I swallowed a week ago at the Jobcentre.

This resembles the beginning of a joke: a man
holding a muleta does not know he is a matador.

Bossman asks of the muleta's worth; if it is silk.
I say it carries the worth of a hungry smile.

Bossman says he will use it as a curtain for the
small window in his bathroom. Instead I offer him

the joke; he refuses, but I tell it to him anyway.

A man holding a muleta
does not know he is a matador,

or that the ground he stands on
is a bullring –

but behind him
is a charging bull

who knows.

Gentle Youth

If retribution was what the youts wanted
not one brick would remain on the city's skyline.
We are over such theatrics – for now.
We browse through the catalogue of anarchy,
underline moments in history, and conclude
that everybody wants to go home.

Who knew the streets was so frail,
could fall apart this easily?
The youts ran in all directions
like scared cattle. Frightened animals
pose the biggest threat, to others
and themselves; basic zoology.

The youts of today are cherry stems
loaded in the magazine
of a gun. The News says us youts will come
for you in the small of the night.
What we really do is [make music, tweet, gram.]
                    unwrinkle nightlight from skin.

One of us saw visions of a new home:
New world, new sky that's so blue it's black too.   *– Frank Ocean*
We are all sat listening to him in tears,
youts robbed of youth, robbed of a rocking cradle,
singing the ballad of the youthful:
If sorrow must come for us / Let it collect us at our homes.

Cold

In that premonition there was bloodbuzz in the air
but we didn't care: we were dripping in sauce,
outfits cold like a Gucci Mane ad-lib: milkflower teeth,
and eyes glossed like the blackest beetle.

Everyone saw us softshoeing in Air Force Ones,
all white like a haunting.
The whole block was rinsed in champagne;
we scrubbed the sky so clean the sparrows thanked us.

Two old men sat outside the newsagent's, talking
about our headline: *2 boys, just 15 –*
one of them Ava's son – so young –
bet they'd never even tasted pussy.

A bloodbuzz stalked the air,
but what more could torment the endz
when its spine already pokes from concrete?
What more, when we look this good gone cold.

Two Bodies Caught in One Cell

A light crawls through the window and folds in on itself
to kneel beside a boy at prayer in a South London police cell.
Of these two bodies, one was there at the Beginning
and since we are all God's children
the two bodies sit as siblings would inside a cell
where no way is up and no side is the right side
and the cell expands, as dark things do, beyond
the reaches of its walls.
                      Walls are the wardens of our justice
and the needle that points to justice is magnetized
by what we are able to sleep with. Sleep
is the third body: the body that is always there
until the light shoos it away
like a shunned sibling, a Cain
found beside the body of an Abel
waiting in a cell, in light, at prayer.

Schrödinger's Black

What are you looting for? asked the evening news, &
the crowd continued looting. I wasn't there, but I thought
I was – my brazen face live on the nation's screens, half-tucked
under a t-shirt chucking bricks. An expert on riots was invited
to speak about why these *particular* young people were rioting.
While he talked they showed more footage:

a bus set on fire,
hooded boys with overgrown nails,
a sky that refused to bring shine nor rain
   (as if it had decided to mind its own business),
a police helmet with a broken visor,
horses clumsy-trotting through piles of debris

– all the chaos and poise of a camp fire story. They showed Mark
Duggan & it was a picture of me even though I wasn't dead. That's
what it feels like to be Black here: like you're dead & alive at the
same time. And though these experts spoke on the mayhem, noth-
ing was said about the maddening of grief. Nothing was said about
loss & how people take and take to fill the void of who's no longer
there. A correspondent in the riot zone asked an old man about
the situation & he said

this time
they demanded payment for death
& so they shook the city down for change

Unsatisfied, she asked a woman, but couldn't make out the words through her accent.

de man ded

Demanded what?

de
man
ded

Survivor's Guilt, or Anikulapo

& so I slipped through the cracks, can't tell you
how it was done: the plain act
of drawing breath each time,
dubbing alternative endings for myself, until
my presence at funerals felt like bragging.

Run over, twice.
Stabbed.
Shot.
A car crash.

I am a museum of all
the ghosts I could have been.
Why me – when better boys
deserved life, when mothers
deserved living sons.

I have sung the chorus of revenge
at red dusk:
Lord, if you be at all, be a blade.   – *Joshua Bennett*
If not, the mandem will do what we must;
though we bow our heads it cannot be for shame.

Gang signs or prayers –
what one cannot solve the other surely will.
My fingers are bilingual like that.
Gun fingers get raised in the dance:
we buss shots up in the clouds.
Angels get hit, & fall like loose feathers.
Sometimes, yeah, mandem forget
& aim into the crowd.

Each dawn I wake
& scroll myself for new scars,
confess that I want to live for good times:
picnic with a peng ting, lips her on the grass.
But every day, on the endz, there is a procession
my breathing body mocks.

III

The Painting On The Concrete Wall

This poem is not about Mike, but let me tell you about him so you know exactly what we are dealing with. 14 years of age, he told us that he'd sold his soul to the Devil & we all laughed. It wasn't that we didn't believe him. Of course we did: we too had seen the Devil in his many faces. We laughed to see Satan get swindled like a rich mark in a brothel because anyone who knew Mike & what he could do when the night air has too much iron in it, knew that that wretched boy didn't have a soul to be marketing out in the first place. This is how Mike became known as Money Mike. But like I said, this poem is not about him.

It is about how one morning we found a painting on the wall of the Winchcombe Court block where Tobi was slapped by that aunty, who has tribal marks long & curved like canoe boats on her cheeks, for spitting on the ground like he didn't have home training. I must admit, on first look, *it* did set my blood to shimmer – I could have shed a *thug tear*. Before long, a crowd gathered at the feet of the painting, neighbours shouting at the windows of other neighbours beckoning them to come out & look. When I close my eyes, I still see the bokeh faces of the families who took portraits on their phones with the painting as a backdrop. Even the council, who could have sent someone to wash the wall back to its concrete greyness, did nothing – as if they too were affected by what the painting had spawned into the air.

Another morning, when a boy from the estate turned 9 years old, he walked out of his 13th-floor flat with a rusty step stool taken from his mother's storage closet. On his descent to ground level, he would stop to collect a gift from each floor: a Pokémon game, a yoyo, small silver coins . . . This was the estate's tradition. I saw the boy set the step stool in front of that painting and lay his gifts out before it until the place looked like a *hood sanctum*. When I asked him, he said it was an offering for his brother's safe return. I said I hadn't seen Mike for many weeks either, and that the body they found in the backseat of a burnt car was too young to have been him. Besides, I said, haven't you heard? Mike has money now, the rich don't die in such ways.

Others must have seen the boy's offering too, and assumed that the painting was the point to register all heavenly enquiries. A woman in a silk head scarf laid a teddy bear on the slab. I fail to recall who left a pint of blue-top milk but the olive oil came from the man who drives the 343 bus. And soon prayers or wishes began to be answered. This neighbour had a debt erased, that once-barren neighbour was now pregnant. The arthritis eased. The back pain was gone. So the step stool grew into a bolstered vigil. Word of the painting's miracles traveled from our endz throughout the city's web of neighbourhoods. From all over, people would come for their share of divine intervention.

Let it not be said that the pensioners of the estate didn't warn the residents that those who strike oil shouldn't go about boasting of its slickness. But what is wisdom when you experience a breakthrough? This is how it was for weeks: people, bent humble, would come to receive and leave. Strangely enough, the boy who turned 9 years old would still sit on his step stool wondering why his brother hadn't been spat out of the sleeve of whatever took him. From first light to night fall, the boy's attendance at the wall stayed consistent – through rain, through shine, through the press photographers and news vans who came once word reached the ears of *TimeOut*'s 'Best New Places to Live', who then brought the deep pockets of those in the business of property to the block. And just like that, we knew what was to come. We, friends of Money Mike, knew the terms of what was to be lost & what was to be gained.

On Magic / Violence

You wouldn't know one from the other
as with all spectacular things.
Who knows what truly goes on in the womb:
is magic the foetus, & violence the umbilical cord?
Did we, in our muggy vision, discard the baby
& rear the afterbirth?

We know the pattern of what begets what,
us poor kids from the block –
experts in both phenomena,
able to point out magic in our bruises,
violence in a rose garden.
When they ask us to speak on it
we will say:
It's a bit of a sticky one still   – Headie One

This will not be enough for them
so they'll force us to put it into words
& we will say:
When hipsters take selfies
on the corners where our
friends died, the rent goes up.

Contrary to Rap Songs a Trap House
Is not All Glitter and Money

*you ain't never been in a nasty 'bando and thought you'd be better
with a 9 to 5*

  – K-Trap

Again, I watch a man eat the entrails of dusk.
That a needle serves as cutlery is not odd, since
anything golden brown can be mistaken for light,
for salvation. Even heroine – especially that.
He says, *Chef got yursef a deal, a free rock every
punter I bring your way*. He knows the others

in the town, grew up here before he moved
to the city to become an investment banker.
I do not know how to pity a white man
who threw away his winning ticket to life.
Besides, nothing of the real world exists
in this house of splitting spirits and bloodshot eyes.

He will make sure I don't wake up if I sleep first.
This is the simple nature of a 'bando.
I saw on the news an MP say, *You'd have
to have no soul to operate in these crack houses.*
But to sit here several days at a time,
after seventeen years of life,

being eyeballed by a vacant face
that dribbles its pain
onto a pus-stained couch, is to watch
my body, flimsy as a bird shot down,

hurtling towards the ground; and my soul
is the only thing left to hold on to.

spirit dancing

harlem shaking

broken glasses

text the group chat

teeth and burners

man turn liars

mad mad angry

spent on casket

then their son sets

why's she crying

as the wind he's

lit house party

two-guns stepping

them man lost it

get the mandem

spark like wires

all those questions

sad sad family

dance at nine night

foolish mother

don't she know that

spirit dancing

ten-toe shuffling

tempers bussing

get your cousin

bring the fire

feds roll up and

but no answers

so much money

'til the sunset

thinks her son's dead

he still lives on

spirit dancing

Concrete Agriculture

& after hunger came anger
& after that we rapped a Giggs verse
& after that we sang the chorus coarse as blackpowder
& an angel

   (an angel is anyone
who visits the desperate
with news)

   told us to pick up what we could
& work the land so we picked up what was scattered
& abundant
& free – we picked up guns
& blades
& pieces of brick
& called them tools to work the land
& when we worked the land, it bore fruits
& we laughed
& after that we sobbed; I tell you the truth: we sobbed
& continued to gorge on the fruits of our work

& If There Is No Other Way,
Long Live The Jugg

If Reece & dem had a clean run
who knows what myth would have said
of their jugg. You know, when Judge gave
them 14 for the ting, Judge's son had to
find a new dealer.

Year before, they brought a white Christmas
to the posh part of the city. 20 bricks in a Ghana-must-go
enough to build a new borough:
we christened them trap ministers.

9/11 changed wholesale prices for real
but the mandem stayed afloat   – *[redacted]*

O trap legends, teach us this buoyancy,
how to become survivors of recessions,
immune to the boom & bust,
the bailiff's bark –
what day isn't a headlock?

Boys in Hoodies

The inside of a hoodie is a veiled nook where a boy pours himself
into a single drop of rain to feed a forest. Each tree grateful for the
wet boy, unaware that the outside world sees this boy as a
      chainsaw.

Have you heard the canned laughter of a chainsaw? Don't listen
      for it
in forests, amid the ankles of trees, or the tongue of dried leaf.

Listen in the vibration of pavements when the concrete is wax,
outside of a Morley's where one chainsaw says to the other,
'member that time when

(gas)

      (gas)

and the money was in his socks?

Then a rip of laughter like the chugger of iron
               or heavy rain
               erupts –

and nearby trees brace for death or life.

Here Too Spring Comes to Us with Open Arms

& it looks like this:

a few *youngers* sprawled like a deck of trick cards on the back
      stairs
talking all that talk about any day now they'll be taken under
      the wing of a dragon

little cousins unseen in the side pocket of the function plotting
      a sleepover
if you ask my mum and I ask yours they'll say yes

twilight and three unbroken voices at the back of the bus
flat earth theories flat asses flat shoes – sweet nonsense chatting

wickedest whine from Chantel and *the boy would've fell on the
      dance floor*
if the arms of his bredrin didn't hold him up (like scaffolding)

two men bouncing along the pavement
through another eye they look like young dolphins slicing coastal
      waves

two schoolgirls walking down the street laughing
nobody knows why

a room of unraveling ribbons reaching for the same microphone
to *spit* over an *eskimo* instrumental

a boy smiles at the mirror welcoming a new strip of muscle
breaking through the sheen of boyishness

a fresh pair of Air Jordans, clean like a smile
and everywhere they touch is hallowed ground

a boy who takes pain like a stone looks up and imagines
stars hanging in the night sky like meditating monks

a girl sends a risky text: the universe gasps and sound falls in
          on itself
a riskier reply is received

at dusk the boy walks through the park
no police no *opps* only the company of spirits

Ode to South Ldn Gyaldem

October is a strange month.
The Sun dies & leaves behind fire petals & you
emerge in the slickest finger waves.
What I would give to see you every night
in my dreams coiling your lower back
like stems slicking around slips of rays,
stopping traffic – traffic-stopping.
I am able to describe the setting to the night
architect who builds my dreams
[October sunset as burning bruise]
but of you, I whisper *memory* & *bronze* &
a long syllable I lose to the tax of waking.
I say you are *unafraid*,
a *roof*: one made of mosaics,
covering a palace somewhere.
I play my favourite natural sound
[sliced plantain stuttering in oil]
I say, *That's it, that's everything I have,*
build me a looping dream of
October's quenching tongue, & you –
you, who can't be made again
in the best work of the night.

Hallelujah Money

Hallelujah money grows from trees
    in the gloomy forest of the estate
        a knife cuts a swinging stem
            the fruit of another yout falls
        Hallelujah! money grows
    for the only funeral parlour
on the endz that tucks
    the decaying fruit into the soil
        to nourish a tree that will someday fruit
           Hallelujah! the funeral director says
        for the fruit of his loins
    don't live on the estate
they get to grow plump and ripe
    and Hallelujah! business is good
        next week another fruit will be
            burst by a bullet – could even be
        a few so they'll do a group discount for them
    the families will say, Hallelujah! at least
the burdensome cost of our child's burial
    is lightened; Hallelujah money is written
                into the headlines of newspapers
        it's the season of the blackest fruit
    exotic piquant body
  what is dead tastes heavenly
so shout it in the church service
        it's time to give Hallelujah money
            to give your tithe – Hallelujah! – it's the seed
        you plant in heaven for the fruit
    of which you'll taste as long as you get in
Hallelujah! says the unknown
    farmer of the land

Hallelujah! they die so young
in this small acre of hell
Hellelujah! Hellelujah! Hellelujah¡

While the Pastor Preached about Hell,
His Son Was Texting Girls

On the left wing of the church,
you sit in rows with the other boys
dressed tidy like a supermarket shelf of tuna
listening to the sermon about a version of Hell:

Burning is Light's work.
You joke to the other boys:
In Naija, burning is light work.

Sometimes the pastor forgets the nature of his congregation
as if Sister Linda's son, who would usually sit behind you,
isn't lying in a ward, half a pound lighter in the liver after
he got caught *slipping* in Brixton.

The congregation knows burning
like it knows childhood photos.

So while the pastor preaches, you text Rachel on your 3310,
peeking at your mother who sits on the other side of church.
You are not met with her usual condemning glare. She sits
pretty like the sequins on her *gele,* facing the clock above

the pulpit and you know she is remembering Jos:
the man who cut the belly of a pregnant woman open
in the street during the riot, fetched the foetus out
and with the cord tied it on a pole to parade.

Your mother believes that this is what
God himself will have to account for –
allowing a man to have such an imagination.

As the sermon continues, only the hands of the clock are heard
ticking a chorus:
>   *Preach of heaven, Pastor;*
>   *we know enough of hell.*

IV

Poor

Night eats day: what more
is there to know about attrition
this is what drove us to learn
how to drive at 14
four boys in a Honda
cheap torque & already better than our
selves of yesterday
the silver finger on the
dashboard said *empty*
– liar: where we come from
empty means dead
& what still moves cannot be empty.

*

By 16 we rolled through streets
blazing music til it could no longer
drown out the engine of our stomachs
thumping.

*

18, we figured it out; in our marrow
knew no bowl would be passed our way.
We eat only by the suppleness of iron
whatever held us before now oxidized
cruising, we mouthed a frenzy to pedestrians
(say it with me
                    say it until you tremble)
night   eats   day   always
what the night touches is carcass

my brother feeds his brother
to *his* enemy because the night . . .
I've seen it – hollow – delicious.

*

We were Pyrex puppies at 19
nourished on hard light
swollen like the fortunate
drifting through the glossy night with
a town crier's bass in our voice
laughing at our 14-year-old selves.
We screamed at people crossing at the lights
(say it with me
                say it until you tremble)

when you get tired of running from danger
you become the danger.

When you get tired of sucking on the void

when you get tired
you become.

Flowering

dem nights when
an oblong of pavement holds
20 closed-petal boys uniformed
in the purpose of riding out
on an *opp's* block, 20 boys
moving to the march of all the
meals they missed to save enough
to buy *110s,* new *kicks* that are
claypots to the stems of 20 boys
on their way to do dirt with thorns
sharpened on the low beams of
their fathers – that's when city
foxes crouch behind silver light.

dem nights when
a traphouse is the basin that holds
all 20 boys as one, to laugh at some
dumb shit that happened *kway* back
in the day or stockpile stories of sex
in estate lifts with girls who lost
a good name for it. that's when
moon water stirs in a Pyrex jug & 20
boys bathe their root ends in dirty talk
because the dirt is what fed the flower
until it was belly-full of grace.

dem nights when
an estate is a pigeonhole shelf
& 20 boys lie in 20 nooks. Cover
them in duvets & call them names
other than Dandelions & they'll dream

– if ghosts ever did – of chalk lines,
hopscotch lines, unlike their
fathers who saw an altar
of pity, of maybes, of *out out*.
that's when 20 open-petal boys,
beautiful as fear, sleep in an
estate, green, everlasting green.

Mandem

If a peacock were a feathered deity, if that deity had
devotees   that would be them over there   bet
over there life is tinged different
       & they see in kaleidoscope
       & sorrow is as hypothetical as the silver rim of clouds
       & they gamble recklessly
       & still win when they lose
       & they've never had a flu or a grazed knee   watch
how they hang low   like gravity doesn't have the nerve
you ever seen a laugh throw sparks?   Keep watching them
over there against the faux limestone looking like a barcode
entangled roses   what will they think of me if I approach with my
own body clutched between my hands   an ill-fitting machine
leaking engine oil
a different sort of slick   black water

Ingredients & Properties of Concrete

INGREDIENTS: cement, sand, tooth of lion, unplucked iris of Saturday, what we will soon come to know as soil, three boys' pact to never forget, dust of vibranium, whispers of the old city, vibration of praise & worship, multicultural London English, debris of a false wall through which black rabbits once vanished, blubber-rich bubblegum, half a blem, milk of magnesia, Grime music, yellow police tape, clingfilm, two truths about death,[1] spilt gourmet kale-and-spinach juice, spilt Supermalt, flakes of beef patty, calcium,[2] batter of a Morley's chicken, bleach.[3]

PROPERTIES: courageousness, sepsis resistance, resistance to drowning, water retention,[4] ability to maintain tensile strength even under the weight of a procession, soundlessness when struck (as paving stone) by the fist of a wailing mother, electrical conductivity,[5] propensity to terraform when in contact with a boy's imagination, shrinkage, creep.[6]

1 One: death is aerodynamic in its coming. Two: death is staccato.
2 From bone or knotweed.
3 So we may start a new day independent of the previous.
4 Beneath the pavement there are rivers of Living water.
5 Electricity is of course the scientific word for anger.
6 The movement of a material in order to relieve stresses within the material, which means, the whole neighbourhood – the whole city – is moving towards the sea.

Concrete (III)

concrete is the lining of the womb
that holds boys with their mothers

when Edvin took a blade to the gut –
bled out like a stream running back to its brook –
concrete held him soft as a meadow might a lamb
so his death looked like a birthing

we who did not know how to weep
raged into the night like the ambulance
that came to lift the empty body
(his mother asked for the sirens to be turned off
lest they disturb her resting boy)

that night we went to chew on the pitchfork of war
so that our grief as if it were a rotting tooth
would be plucked out

Community

fuckinnnn who's chatting shit? / I'll bang you in the throat if you're chatting shit / fucking bounce your head off the concrete / you know what? what endz you from? / this is my block / my fucking endz / mine / fucking mine / you'ge'me / you can't pass thru my bits / do you know who man is? / man's mashed work on the block / done dirt / walking around like you're bad / you're not bad / I'm bad / I'll show you bad / show you crud / who you know on this block / mandem? / fuck you and your mandem / true say you look like a fed / you a fed / on some obbo shit / so what you doing on my block then? / what you doing here / what you want round here / who your cousin round here / who your aunty / who your old man always drunk off dragon stout / who your weed shotter / who your postman talking everyone's business / who your broke man always asking to borrow a fiver / who your washed-up older / who your four baby moms with another on the way / who your got deported and came back again / who your I could have been a footballer but I hurt my knee / who your uncle with sad eyes / who your family that make all the noise / who your family with a hundred kids / who you know here that ain't here no more / who your shifty eyes judging through curtains / who your girl who is in uni now / who your old woman that still gives you lemon sweets / who you know on this block blud? / so what you doing on my block / what you fucking doing here?

Trauma Is a Warm Bath

Just ask the boy who carries anger on his
shoulders like two canons; blastoise bold,
hardened like old eyes that know
how wasteful it is to cry in a drought.
Who took another boy's life at a funeral.

Often he would tell the shiny version to a girl
who cornrowed his hair on her living room floor.
She would hear of how he pulled the trigger *easy;*
like turning off a bathroom light switch.
She knew there was too much theatre in his voice,
decided to run him a bath and told him,
When you can no longer shrug that day away
the bosom of a warm bath will see you through.

Just ask the paramedic at the scene:
he knew the body was shoebox empty
but all his training didn't tell him what to do
when a boy gets shot at a funeral, and the crowd
are unwilling to ration bowed heads
between the two dead bodies.
How bizarre it is to give CPR to a vacant body
for 30 minutes; his sorriest apology.

Just ask the mother who worked
until her hands curled like boiled crabs
to have a son on safer shores; fed him;
bought him toothpaste for two decades, almost.
Who would get a call that said she had birthed
her son into a casket after all.

Just ask the boy writing this poem
who feels *like death is a party*
all his friends were invited to but him,
who scribbles the name of his dead friend
on paper. He thinks the paper is a Ouija board;
he thinks a poetry reading is a séance.
What a farce! Expecting the dead to speak
in the voice of the living.

How to Pronounce: Peckham

After Nate Marshall's 'pronounce'

pek

fold your lips like uniform of *dead* boy
parents said it was when he was most
happy so they buried him in it along with 24
classmates' colouring pencils
not the right kind of stick that'll keep at bay
the jaws that speak the news (*another one dead . . . look . . . see)*
how the mourning hangs in the air as thick as pollen
& like all fevers not everyone is affected
Mrs George (flat beneath us) who can't hear too good & turns
the volume up to max for *Countdown* says
it's a shame what you people do to each other

now punch the sound through your nose
even if the nasal passage clasps
like the fingers around a bottle
of brothers
who didn't think
he would *actually die . . .*

nărm

this time the tongue leans on the roof of the mouth
like winter on the shoulder of these blocks trying
to catch its breath
the right place to find a really bad day

we watched a Vietnam war film
& saw a regular Tuesday
just more confetti
& though their trenches weren't
suspended corridors like ours
the gist was the same

Peckham [pek narm]

The Moon Gave no Name
to Tides

Yesterday, another boy took your name –
back of Rockingham Estate.
What's in a name? That thing
that latches itself to the undercut of your ribs,
convinces you it is your liver?
What are you to do without one,
and what is another boy doing with two?

You go to get it back,
take a shotgun the length of your torso.
At the trial, your father will testify
about the family name,
its reputation back in Warri;
how your grandfather often played the
mediator, famous for his sayings:

Water get no enemy.
If it drowned your child
you still have to drink it, bathe with it.
It is better to take up a grudge
with the moon: the moon
makes the water rise and fall.

As your father leaves the witness box,
the prosecutor – teeth
the colour of sheep –
turns to you, and says,

Perhaps, young man,
you should have shot at the moon.

Two Seconds Before the Trigger Is Pulled

[01:43:12]

A gun is held to the back of a boy's head;
its handler sits at the feet of his god.

He has become his own furnace,
thinks he understands the big joke of power:

a mountain is not so imposing
when the bullet, the birthright of faith, makes it move.

Meanwhile, pigeons flutter and coo,
waiting for the barrel to ring.

[01:43:12]

What is given can be taken away: this is
the perimeter line of our life's small domain.
So the boy takes in a gulp of air hoping
it kills him before the gun can,
because that too is power – that too
is drawing a border between head & barrel
& ushering in a demise of his choosing.

[01:43:13]

When the trigger is pulled

the handler will be pulled too

– his skeleton pulled

from the meat of his body;

he will become a breakable core, brittle

as his mother would describe the wailing infant

she'd given to this blue Earth.

The handler does not know this.

The trigger is pulled.

[01:43:13]

The weapon jams   God laughs

Just kidding   *just kidding*

V

The Book of the Generation of Peckham Boys

*from the Sons of Yellow Brick
to the Sons of Crane*

After Matthew I

Peckham Boys begat Marlon & Marlon begat Raver & Raver begat Younger Raver and his brethren the YPBs & Younger Raver begat Fighter & Fighter begat Younger Fighter until that business about the missing re-up money & so Younger Fighter begat X-Fighter and his brother Smasher in exile who then begat Younger Smasher the diplomat & Younger Smasher lay with the sister of Younger Raver to beget The Weeping Wall Glossed in RIPs /

& The Weeping Wall Glossed in RIPs begat Tiny Raver and the YYPBs & Tiny Raver when he became a Birthing Tree on the Old Kent Road begat Ruthless the daughter of after rain & Ruthless met a knife in her heart & so the streets bled & begat Dead-song & Dead-song begat The Uncle plucking coins from the ear back of the estate & The Uncle begat Diamond and his brother Timmy & Diamond begat Younger Butcher who swallowed a gun &

Younger Butcher begat Tiny Butcher who spat out bullets & Tiny Butcher begat Tiny Giggler and the Shurland Massive & the Shurland Massive begat PYG who spewed out mayhem at their circumcision & PYG begat a thousand epilogues named Y.O.T & Y.O.T begat the Word /

& the Word begat Beginning and her brother Fullness & Fullness begat Foulness & Foulness begat a Zoo of headlines & a Zoo begat Damilola & Damilola begat Dew on the closing petal of evening & Dew begat Final Fear of who begat the One Who Reads This – yes, you – who then begat Me.

THE STORY OF MARLON

Somewhere in his lineage
a bad sacrifice was offered
to Elohim. How else could
Marlon explain the luck
the men of his family knew?
It takes a hellish grudge
to wage a war on heaven.
When the police finally
caught up with him, it is said
he was laden with ammunition
– enough to take on God.

THE STORY OF RUTHLESS

Anyone smart enough
to study the food chain
of the estate knew exactly
who this warrior girl was;
once she lined eight boys
up against a wall,
emptied their pockets.
Nobody laughed at the boys.

Something about August makes bugs
& boys gather in numbers.

(It would be lazy
to blame it on the heat.)

At Shurland Gardens their faces
were smooth like weeping pebbles,
skin smelling of distant shorelines,
theatrical in their play.

I swear you could watch them for hours.

The same children
labelled *thugs* & *crooked*
forced trees
that bend to eat sunlight.

In those days, Goodness & Mercy
followed us every day of our lives
as long as we dwelled in Dominic's house
on Sunday afternoons, around the time
his Mum (church Head Caterer)
would dish us moist portions: jollof,
curry goat, plantain & all. We would eat
while she hummed a benediction
& we would leave full in body & in spirit.

You needed to see him move.
It was like a swan in tame water:
pirouette. Plié. Pirouette. Fatality.
He wore a long, black coat with a hood.
Said he wanted to be known as Zorro.
Sure enough, to his face he was called
just that. But each time a new back
was laid out on the ground
and we went to spread the news, only
the brilliant violence of an X
could title his legend.

Me was born with his embryonic sack
still intact. *This happens only when*
they remember their previous life,
said the nurse. *They reenter the world*
already cautious; bones resistant.
It is better to have a child this way –
one who is prepared.

THE STORY OF BEGINNING

Like her brother Fullness,
she had a birthmark freckled
across her collarbone.
Anything that could rise at dawn
would not – without her say-so.
Sometimes Venus lingered out
a little while past night, into
the dawn, to catch a glimpse.

THE STORY OF DEAD-SONG

Bruv – don't hold back
Love – don't show that
I used to show love in the hood
But the same love never got shown back

A happy boy lived and his warmth filled the corridors of the block.
Go well where you go, boy with a smile like a burning chariot.

THE STORY OF THE UNCLE PLUCKING COINS
FROM THE EAR BACK OF THE ESTATE

If you heard him whistle *O when the saints,*
you knew it was a woeful day at the bookies
and the ripest time for us, hanging outside the block,
to play him at *money up.* He would always oblige
whether drunk or sick

                          and clean us out in one sweep:
seven tails, a Yoda grunt, then ascend the stairs,
singing *O when the saints.*

VI

Repress

'immune privilege': the outside of your eye prevents your immune system from knowing about the inside of your eye. If it didn't, your immune system would destroy your eyes.

that time I was in a hospital bed & death drifted
through the ward like a gardener
checking on the ripeness of his plants
inspecting each body attached to vines
& two detectives stood
like cherubs
on either side of me

tell us exactly what you saw

I saw milk
dripping
from the udder of a car
traces of diesel
the sky a locked gate
I could not ascend
reeking of gravity

so did you see who shot you?

yes I saw his touch
its pulse like my father
who held me twice
the day I was born
the day I angered him

we need you to describe his face, can you do that?

I saw smoke
puncture
the heart of an ugly future
his aura thick
as the lip of his gun
its one loose tooth

unhelpful they said this is unhelpful
I told them the issue was medical
that I was cocooned inside of my mind's eye
locked out on the verandah of my memory
unable to see the incident
that had nearly destroyed me
the memory that surely would

Remembrance

how often we forget that tomatoes are fruit
what more do we misremember of a house
once as a boy   angered by my mother
I paced up & down like a warden in our kitchen
until the rage was too much for me to hold
in my green body   picked up a butter
knife & stabbed the Bible   kept centre
in the dining table   nobody saw
though the walls drained of their chic blue
windows stiffened   lachrymose to this day
the scar on the leathered sleeve
remains   unquestioned like the scriptures held
within   as each breakfast I tried to forget
parts of myself   spoonful by spoonful . . .

so the house   what kindness of a house to fold
memories away   to allow us to call
ourselves what we think we are
pastor's son   the example   hearer of His word

does a house speak   yes   creaks on the
staircase   the living room   an infantry
of syllables   a dislocated sentence to the impatient
ear   *I will keep all*
of your unwanted memories here   & here
                & here

& here

The First Time You Hold A Gun

I held it in my hands: it was soft
like my mother's teet. My gums
still remembered that sensation,
and gave my hands the memory.

Amid the dull chiming of an evening light
I sat as a beggar boy would, knowing

the press of metal heavy in my palms,
near my own as a new-born; my spine
remembered the weight of my infant body
and gave my hands the memory.

As I moved to tuck it into a corner
dark enough to muffle its blushing coat,

I sensed it glint between my fingers, shimmering
like my mother's skin during a cradle song;
my eyes remembered the view from a cot,
and gave my hands the memory.

One thing must be given for one thing:
that is the nature of bartering.

Now all that is   soft
                             weighted
                             shimmering
carries the echo of a   gun
and not my   mother.

Patrilineal

my father lives with his head inside a blood orange
he, unassuming in frame, would tell me
of the fathers who came before me
how his father died   after he touched *his* father's beard
this is one of two things I know of my forefathers
when he would beat me I would study him in action, belt
swinging like a skipping rope from his shoulder to my arm
or back or buttocks   belly   he would beat the part of
himself in me   beating some unhatched omen away
away   away & I performed
sobbing to appease his urge to exorcise

my mother & siblings are Arsenal fans   it is only I
who chose Man Utd   my father's club   I hoped that he
would see me the way a teammate sees another on the grass
at dinner it is always a winter night & we serve portions
of our faces   our brown eyes   prickly & gorgeous
we speak only of matches & the Word

once when there was no football   to survive
the silence   I told him I dreamt a prophecy
& began to prophesy every unescaped thing in his throat
things that made him afraid of him   & me for knowing &
speaking it all out into the world   when I no longer knew
what to say   I coughed up a half-eaten eyeball & told him it
was just my hay fever   playing up again

Concrete (IV)

When everyone called me son of a shadow
it was concrete that called me proof of light.

Behind my block Kaysha said she liked Ashton:
my legs gave way and I sunk into the wall.

For a brief moment, I was the marrow of concrete,
marking my pain there against its texture.

When I was younger, I'd played with Ashton. We drew
the future in chalk; and hopscotch, goal posts, faces.

That was when I felt safe on concrete: at least
the devil couldn't breach the ground.

I wish once again to be haunted by a simpler agent.
Back then I knew who I hated and loved;

now concrete has made an equilibrium of me.
I am no more a good insulator – I don't hold on

to the hate or Kaysha's scent or my own chest.
Come winter, the cold wind will pass through me.

It will pass like notes through the clef of a sugared song,
like sound through an ear that will not hear.

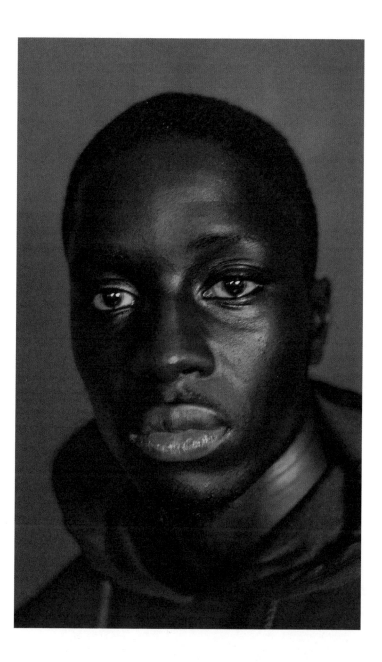

A Designer Talks of a Home /
A Resident Talks of Home (II)

00:23:12   I grew up in a part of London that was filled with
            derelict houses. To see that a building could have such
            an impact on the way people felt . . . on the way they
            interacted

00:33:13   *the lift never works so you take the stairs . . . sometimes*
            you pass your neighbours and catch up on the news

00:24:03   you really need to choose materials that are functional
            yet luxurious

00:33:19   *like the other day I see man like Tevin in a Gucci*
            tracksuit, Egyptian cotton, with the Belincies. He looked

00:24:15   the beauty of these things

00:34:12   *mad stressed, ain't seen him since he started linking*
            that rich girl

00:24:21   this is a place to make them feel human

00:35:02   *stayed at her place for two weeks said he didn't mean*
            to . . . her pillows were goose feather

00:25:12   we understand materials best by contrast; rough feels
            rougher by contrast with smooth

00:36:13   *said her mates kept calling him Tyrone . . . one asked if*
            he stabbed someone before & everyone laughed . . .
            didn't answer . . . next morning his girl asked him again

00:25:37   less about aesthetics or appearance

00:37:24   *a Gucci tracksuit just looked like a regular tracksuit when Tevin wore it [laughter]*

00:26:03   but much more about making an environment that made people feel better after they had been there than when they arrived

00:38:06   *said he felt strange every day he stayed at her place*

00:26:23   it's about when people walk in there they don't know why they feel the way they feel

00:39:01   *couldn't put his finger on it just knew he couldn't stay there ever again*

00:26:35   it's actually all been orchestrated

00:40:39   *[inaudible]*

00:26:57   design that encourages people to be close together is a good thing

00:42:04   *went back to the one bedroom flat he shares with his mum, dad & four siblings*

Yard

all the [houses]
I have lived in sit in my ribcage
with faces like beggars
I dream my postmortem
unzip my skin & ask each [house], *what
are you: a mother, a sculptor, a motionless meadow?*

I take myself on a tour through my self
each circle of [house] is visited
you see this [house] here under my left lung
it taught me to eat with my mouth closed
in this one-down at my right calf
I did not know how beautiful the evening
sun was until it painted the walls
in this one I was a magician; in this one, a king
of a shabby kingdom & my subjects were bony
there nobody asked me to prove shit
asked why was I was standing where I was standing
or if I had an offensive weapon on me
I could not feed anyone a supper but I
kept love in this [house] – the old thing
I kept a shoobs invited the whole endz to this
cramped corner of the world we grew enormous
yak spilled on skirts air ached with sweet sweat
daggering gyal zoots ashed on my windowsill
I held a shoobs every night they swaggered
back like the legs of tarantulas swimming through
the dark we supped on this only
between songs we christened this [house]
NEW BLACK[HOUSE] or [HOUSE] OF COMMONS

kept eight buckets of water in the [house]'s eight corners
because there were enough of us in there to die by fire

East Dulwich Road

When a knife enters you, there will be no pain.
People on the street & on buses will stare
as if witnessing a natural phenomenon.
They will imagine the pain they think you are in
but you will feel none at all.

You will question if you have always been
an empty cove waiting to be filled by another boy's rage.
Whether this is how mutation works; whether, after generations,
your black body now accepts the blade with comfort,
like an inheritance – a birthmark on your obsidian torso.

The Six

Six stabbings in an hour is nothing
to write about. Nonetheless, this is what we learned:

that the mother called other mothers to check
it wasn't their sons only to find out it was hers.

That aside from the six, on the other side
of the city, one brother killed the other.

That the Earth, unbroken horse,
wants us off her back.

That the dark palm of probability
demands a toll on our lives.

That one in every clutch of us
must take a bullet or a blade.

That in this chapter of British violence
the nation shivers

with its face hidden
when questions are asked:

of the dead: aren't you satisfied?
of the living: aren't you grateful?

of the politician: aren't you ashamed?
of the heavens: aren't you replenished?

[redacted]phobia

I want you to know that we are scared but not because of you.
We've seen guns you brought here. We've seen knives you placed
    in our palms.
We've seen your Jesus as a baby & a man. We've seen your Mary
broken – pious. We've seen your carnival of legions. We know
what chokes in the shadows; & if we don't know its name,
we know you do. We've seen you lock doors, clutch your bag,
grip onto your children. We know the history you crafted. We've
    seen
your culling. We know what happens when you tell us to smile
& relax. When we close our eyes & count to ten, we know
what happens when we open them again. We've seen burning.
We've seen streamlining. We've seen your crack. We've seen
the back of police vans. We know the end of batons. We've tasted
the sting of tasers. We know courtrooms. We've heard *guilty*
& sentencing. We know all the years by days. We've numbered
fewer bredrins every other sunrise. We've read all of your
    headlines
& everything you've said about us. We know your [redacted].
We know your ways, your cruel ways, and see no shame in
    admitting it.
We are scared, it's true: but it is not because of you.

Excerpts from Journal Entries, 2017

This morning, I wake up to the tweets and posts about a burning tower. I am reading the posts as if they are in real time: 11pm 'that estate next to . . .', 1am 'It hasn't stopped'. I am watching it in the present, from the future. People are burning and dying and I am in the future, stuck. And so I do what the helpless do when they first realise they are helpless: I cry. I cry and keep scrolling, watching more videos, and the tears smudge my sight so I can only hear the people and the night. The screen of my phone bends away from me. *Stop, I can't show you more.* But I force it to because I can't sit alone with this grief. [In the future, every time I write *grief* on my phone its autocorrect asks if I mean *Grenfell*: have I written Grenfell so many times that it has registered it as a familiar word, or is this how collective mourning works?] My mind is a rolodex of all the fires I have seen on the estate I grew up in, but I think, this will be it, surely, this is the turning point where everything changes, where people will listen and laws will change and trucks will come loaded with solutions. [I am in the future and nothing has.] What is there left to do? I am learning the map of spite like I am learning the map of a lover. I know now what it means to truly hate. But I do not know who I hate: is it the man who commented 'I would actually feel bad for him if he didn't sound like such a roadman . . .' under a news clip where a resident boy talks about losing his friends and neighbours, demanding answers from the Government? Or is it the Government, or is it the News channels, sipping on the ripe mourning of the poor?

Many nights I have dreams that the Earth has rolled her oceans over and decided to start again. As I sink into her waters I think, good for you. They have learned to make a business out of trage- dy, now that even death is powerless to hold the imagination. In another clip, there is a Black guy talking about how he almost died in the fire and how a little boy, an immigrant man and others died in the smoke, and I am angry that people get to see this, people who don't give a shit get to see this, get to listen to his trauma like pub chatter.

My people, my poor people, my browner people, my *other* people who are not seen as people, they do not inspire moral shame in those who govern this place, this is a song I have come to know too well. If those in the higher seats of the high places don't note Grenfell as a mass murder, as gross incompetence, as a final warning, as a regression of Humanity then they should at the very least take note (since they all watched it from their windows) of the nature of a spreading fire: if the bottom burns then surely with time the top will, too. Surely it will succumb to the flames.

VII

On the Other Side of the Street

I crossed over
& now the hood won't take me back.
I stink of uptown, high ceilings, grand windows –
they know that I room in the belly of the bourgeois.
They can smell it all on me:
how I dance in the banquet halls
saying I am hungry, and though this was true once,
I say it like it still means what it meant
before I swapped my hood pass for weightlessness.
I say *hungry* now for *greedy*,
devour pastures on pastures.
My skin has lost its tinge of blue from police lights
but the mandem are kind to me for old times' sake.
Now, they let me in the room
with strict instructions:
no dancing
no laughing
nothing to be passed my way
no yak
no blunts.
They say I flavour the air with pseudo-celebration;
that it *feels mad bookie* when they call out
for God's face amid the milky smoke.
They fear now that God might just show up
& ruin everything.

Old New

I wake up rooted
in the good part of Hackney
am I accepted

Or just too brutal
for the brutalist elbow
bone-filled alleys now

Sinless brick limewash
streets clean like repentance
the old drugs have left

the new drugs classy
the OD hits different
powder decorum

New drugs modernist
new drugs Nicaraguan
ornamental pond

You can't say CRACK here
you'll fuck the house prices
what you say is craquè

Ballad for the Baddest Yout On The Endz

After Shiro's 'Woodpecker Lullaby'

O sad little woodpecker,
drilling the face of the estate,
staining the cold concrete, stretching

your woeful story across our windows –
you have coloured our mornings,
flightless and alone. You sing of how

an angry old god turned your beak
into a poisoned blade
that stained your whole endz blue;

how, now your touch brings with it toxins,
friends who come near you
end up buried at your feet.

O little woodpecker,
you know nothing of rain,
only the tears that run
between your nylon feathers.

The Watcher

After Jesse James Solomon, 'Strata'

I see the painting / I see a young me / I see the foxes / they eat
a bagel / look through the window / I see the frost leaves / I see
their bronze tips / I see the police / doing a strip search / the sun
is hiding / I see the moonlight / coming to save them / a field of
pavement / crying canaries / I heard it's bad luck / I see the chaos
/ it could be Rembrandt / could be Re-nay-sance / Ethiopian /
Iconography / I see the faces / praying for daybreak / I want to help
them / I'm just a watcher / sat on my bus seat / led by a stranger /
I want to help these / epochs of brief things / their tears are seep-
ing / into the canvas / souls of descendants / heart of a rich man /
wounded & bleeding / could be a mistake / smudge of the oil / is it
sgraffito / say it's graffiti / the night is teething / cos I can feel it /
gnawing my eyeballs / so now I listen / and hear the painting / and
hear a trumpet / and hear a trumpet / I hear the trumpet / thefin-
altrumpet /thefinaltrumpet/thefinaltrumpet/

At a House Party, 'Ultralight Beam' Came on & It Started a Church Service

& in the corner, two spiders
watched us entranced
by the words of a little girl
pouring through the speakers
like anointing oil

*

One spider said to the other, *This is how
they exalt so be careful; they'll not notice
treading on you*: & the other spider said, *Yes
we are watching our devils
pray away their devils.*

*

The bass made your eyes heavy
like that time with the mandem
in a Vauxhall ringer, hotboxing –
searching for a name
the streets would know you by.

*

Things with names deserve deliverance.
That's why you don't name the spiders
you find scuttering across your kitchen floor:
otherwise, your house becomes a sanctuary.

*

The name given to you by your father
is not your right name. It is your occupation
in this world – determines how many friends
you will have, how many of your CVs will be discarded
without a glance, how much Justice you will be afforded,
how many lovers will think twice
before they introduce you
to their families; how much money you will make, ever.

*

Did you know that God takes down the names
of everyone who pays their tithe,
everyone who says His name in vain?
– That there is a book in which the names are kept
of all who will see Paradise.

We Will Not All Fight like Dogs at Our Death

I have never loved anything the way I love the endz.
On a good day – not necessarily a sunny one –
I whisper wicked things into its ear,
charge the air with electricity.

Aunty said she knew by the way I played
with the other kids I would grow to be a jealous lover.
I am not yet grown & I have chosen to love something
nobody wants to love – that nobody can truly be loved by.
I am on course to defy Aunty's prediction.

I know this much:
we are all going to die
in this dunya.

If anything should kill me, let it be
the starchy bass of passa in front of the yard-food shop;
let it be the piercing mutter of mandem on pedal bikes,
grating against brick walls . . .
(Yes, it is strange to order your own death like takeaway.)

I've never spoken to my father about love.
If I did, I imagine his advice would be this:
Learn to love what everyone sees as ugly.

Isn't that the ethos of love in all tragedies?
Toxic, ritualistic, taxing of
at least one of every two lives?
Yet I dance the terrible dance of love,
surrendering myself to the pulse of street lamps:

To die for the dust of your land is purest.
We will not all fight like dogs at our death.
Some of us will lay on the grass, green like
in cartoons, shoeless, & with our arms
held out for love's embrace.

Concrete (V):
Second Anniversary

Breathe in the morning air: today of all days
this concrete is a field of soluble petals
purple to the stem.
Activate your sharingan, my g:
where you're standing is much more than you know.

Breathe in & tell the mandem I remain
flourishing & sublunary
just like the stories promised ghosts would be.
Tell them I smell like that day we hid
from feds for 6 hours in the bakery.

There is no flash flood coming.
Breathe in
chaos, & breathe out my soft limbs –
& if you wish me to speak
I will.

LIST OF IMAGES

All images are the original work of the author.

NOTES

'A Designer Talks of a Home / A Resident Talks of Home' (I) and (II) are found poems; the designer's lines rework dialogue from *Ilse Crawford, Interior Designer*, episode 8 of the documentary series *Abstract: The Art of Design* (Netflix, 2017).

'Because of the Times' is for the former residents of North Peckham Estate. The epigraph is taken from John Boughton's *Municipal Dreams: The Rise and Fall of Council Housing* (Verso Books, 2018).

In 'Gentle Youth', the quotation is taken from Travis Scott's 'Carousel' featuring Frank Ocean.

'Schrödinger's Black' is for Mark Duggan (RIP).

In 'Survivor's Guilt, or Anikulapo', the quotation is taken from Joshua Bennett's poem 'Still Life With Black Death'.

In 'On Magic / Violence', the quotation is taken from Headie One's interview with NFTR (GRM DAILY, Youtube, 2018).

In 'Contrary to Rap Songs a Trap House Is not All Glitter and Money', the epigraph is taken from K-Trap's 'Paper Plans'.

'[spirit dancing]' is for Conrad Barnes-Worrell.

'Ode to South Ldn Gyaldem' is for my WCW.

'Poor' is for T.O.S and C-Block.

'Trauma Is a Warm Bath' is for Azezur (H) Khan (RIP).

'How to Pronounce: Peckham' is for Damilola Taylor (RIP).

In 'The Moon Gave no Names to Tides', the epigraph is taken from Dizzee Rascal's 'Respect Me'.

'The Book of The Generation of Peckham Boys . . . ' is for the Narm.

In 'Repress', the epigraph is inspired by Kierstan Boyd's article 'The Eye and Immune Privilege' published on the American Academy of Ophthalmology website (aao.org, 2018).

'At a House Party, "Ultralight Beam" Came on & It Started a Church Service' is for SXWKS.

'Concrete (V): Second Anniversary' is for Edvin Johnson.

ACKNOWLEDGEMENTS

I am grateful to Natalie Teitler. I am grateful to Roger Robinson, Jacob Sam-La Rose, Nick Makoha and Malika Booker who all saw in me a potential I didn't see in myself. To Sharmilla Beezmohun, Sarah Saunders, Joy Francis, Lisa Mead, Bohdan Piasecki, Aliyah Hasinah, Suzanna Alleyne. Grateful to my family: my mother and father. My siblings who I infinitely love: Shola, Toyin, Esther and Joshua. My beautiful nieces.

Shout out to my SXWKS dons who have always championed me: Lex, Olivia, Aiden, Abu, Kush, Charles, Nardia, Sarah, Marta, Barbara, Naya, Jolade, Dillon, Darius, Jake, Rui, Haja, Afoma, Sophia, Ordella, Jordan, Josette, Keziah, Julian, Siobhan, Remi and Ruth. Shout out to the mandem from endz: Rem, Jud, Mig, Jimmy, George, Seon, Jordan, Bukky, David. Shout out to Dan Saraki, Jojo Sonubi, Dillon Kalyabe, Genevieve, Jack Gillian, Ned, Sumia, Hibaaq, Layla, Nana, Jesse Bernard, Franklyn, Lionheart, Jemilea Wisdom-Baako, Malakai Sergeant, Yakubo, Tyrone Lowe, Susanna, Emmanuel Sugo, Shade Joseph, Adeyemi Michael, Nancy Adimora, Jumoké Fashola.

I am grateful to the following people for helping me to become a better writer: Max Porter, Jane Commane, Kayo Chingonyi, Ilya Kaminsky, Mimi Khalvati, Polar Bear, Nii Ayikwei, Theresa Lola, Richard George.

I am thankful to Ruth Harrison, Paul Sherreard, Patrice Lawrence, Tom Andrews and the rest of the STW team. Thank you to Rachel Mann and to Suresh Ariaratnam.

Thank you to all the poetry nights that have invited me to read.

I am grateful to the following magazines and journals, where some of these poems have appeared, often in different forms: *Glamcult, Wasafiri, Ink Sweat and Tears, London Magazine, The Capilano Review, Dazed & Confused, ASOS magazine, The Guardian, Litro Magazine, Somesuch.*

Big shout out to Yomi Sode; every time.

I am grateful to the Arts Council whose funding made this book possible.